A Way of the Cross

A Way of the Cross

In *Communion* with *Creation*

Christine Kresho, CSJ

Paulist Press
New York / Mahwah, NJ

Scripture quotations are from *New Revised Standard Version Bible: Catholic Edition*, copyright © 1989, 1993 National Council of the Churches of Christ in the United States of America. Used by permission. All rights reserved worldwide.

Cover image by Elena Terletskaya/Shutterstock.com
Cover and book design by Lynn Else

Library of Congress Cataloging-in-Publication Data
Names: Kresho, Christine, author.
Title: A way of the cross: in communion with creation / Christine Kresho, CSJ.
Description: New York/Mahwah, NJ: Paulist Press, [2025] | Summary: "This book invites us to pray with the forever Christ still suffering in our brothers and sisters today in union with all creation awaiting redemption"—Provided by publisher.
Identifiers: LCCN 2024028807 (print) | LCCN 2024028808 (ebook) | ISBN 9780809157310 (paperback) | ISBN 9780809188994 (ebook)
Subjects: LCSH: Stations of the Cross.
Classification: LCC BX2040 .K73 2025 (print) | LCC BX2040 (ebook) | DDC 232.96/3—dc23/eng/20240807
LC record available at https://lccn.loc.gov/2024028807
LC ebook record available at https://lccn.loc.gov/2024028808

ISBN 978-0-8091-5731-0 (paperback)
ISBN 978-0-8091-8899-4 (ebook)

Published by Paulist Press
997 Macarthur Boulevard
Mahwah, NJ 07430
www.paulistpress.com

Printed and bound in the
United States of America

Opening Prayer

O Jesus, you came to live on this earth so God might become visible to us, that we might glimpse the mystery of the one who created us and all that exists. You invited us to follow you, promising that your path would free us and all of creation from the bondage of decay into the glorious freedom of God's beloved. As we remember your way, we pray with gratitude that you carry the cross with us as we endure the cost of discipleship with you.

Option 1: If you are using this in your parish or with a small group you may want to use a refrain such as "Jesus, remember me when you come into your kingdom" as the leader or group moves to the next station.

Option 2: For a group setting or personal use, a scripture passage is offered for silent reflection.

Station One

Jesus is condemned to death

We adore you, O Jesus, who formed us in love and calls us to follow you.

Jesus speaks:

O Spirit, alive within me, I groan with all your creation as we face condemnation. My heart breaks for all your children who suffer the pain of hatred, exclusion, violence, and suspicion. I weep with our planet as it gasps for breath. I long to embrace all your creatures, those who swim in the depths, those who soar above the trees, those so small they are rarely seen, and those so large they stir us with their awesome strength or beauty. Death engulfs the hope for redemption, yet faith connects us to you, Spirit of Love.

We respond:

We pray for the courage to see you, O God of Life, in all that threatens us with destruction. We beg you to enlighten us, strengthen us, encourage us to choose life for ourselves and all of creation. Redeem us, O God, our faithful One.

Scripture reflection:

"We know that the whole creation has been groaning in labor pains until now; and not only the creation, but we ourselves, who have the first fruits of the Spirit, groan inwardly while we wait for adoption, the redemption of our bodies." Romans 8:22–23

Station Two

Jesus carries his cross

We adore you, O Jesus, who formed us in love and calls us to follow you.

Jesus speaks:

My God, the Creator of all that is and has been, strengthen me as I pick up my cross. I hear bitter cries from my earthly home; I look at so many faces drenched in tears as senseless violence takes away their loved ones. The sun is darkened by clouds of thick smoke; the forests are ablaze, and the glaciers are melting. The voices of prophets plead for ears to listen and hearts to be opened. The struggles are so great but in hope we beg you, Creator God, to renew the face of the earth and to entrust us again with resurrection.

We respond:

We pray to be empowered by love for all you have created, O wondrous God. Open our eyes to your Sacred

Presence inviting us to embrace all that you have so graciously given as gifts to be treasured. Breathe into us new life so that we may rightly care for all that belongs ultimately to you.

Scripture reflection:

"But, in accordance with [God's] promise, we wait for new heavens and a new earth, where righteousness is at home." 2 Peter 3:13

Station Three

Jesus falls the first time

We adore you, O Jesus, who formed us in love and calls us to follow you.

Jesus speaks:

O Wisdom, who danced with joy at the beginning of creation, lift me up with all those who dream and wait for new birth. When frustrations, disappointments, and failures tempt us to forget your vision for wholeness, give us hope to rise again. Help us remember that we are one in you and, therefore, are bound to care for each other. Convince us, O Wisdom, to continue the journey as sons and daughters of the one and same God.

We respond:

We commit ourselves to trusting your faithfulness to us and to all of creation. We dare to accept your desire that we be co-creators as we assume responsibility for the lives of each other and the continued existence of our planet.

We pray in gratitude for your ongoing creating power that sustains each and every part of creation.

Scripture reflection:

"When [the Creator] marked out the foundations of the earth, then I was beside [God], like a master worker; and I was daily [God's] delight, rejoicing before [the Sacred One] always, rejoicing in [God's] inhabited world and delighting in the human race." Proverbs 8:29–31

Station Four

Jesus meets his afflicted mother

We adore you, O Jesus, who formed us in love and calls us to follow you.

Jesus speaks:

As I look into the agonized eyes of my mother, I see the anguish of all mothers. Out of their depths of despair I hear them wail for the children who are no more. I grieve for the hopes and dreams that you, their Maker, had planted within their beautiful minds. I weep over the fragile bodies you had so elegantly designed now shattered and broken into pieces no longer recognizable. I cry for all the lost talents and gifts they could have contributed to your ever-expanding creation.

We respond:

O Creator God, teach us how to treasure all those you have given us to love. Open our eyes to the unique value inherent in every child you have woven in the wombs of their mothers. We pray that we will see your Divine light in their eyes and bow to your sacred Spirit alive within their being.

Scripture reflection:

"But we have this treasure in clay jars, so that it may be made clear that this extraordinary power belongs to God and does not come from us." 2 Corinthians 4:7

Station Five

Simon helps Jesus carry his cross

We adore you, O Jesus, who formed us in love and calls us to follow you.

Jesus speaks:

I am grateful that Simon's help lightens my burden and I wonder if anyone remembers what I told them about your constant care and protection. When they see flowers in bloom, do they think of your fatherly work that cultivates their beauty? When a bird falls to the ground, are they aware of your motherly compassion holding its brokenness? Will they learn to lessen the pain endured by their brothers and sisters? Will they answer the distress of the planet being crushed by the weight of dominion and neglect?

We respond:

O God, you have given us eyes to see and ears to hear. Help us feed the hungers in our world and unite ourselves with all who struggle to walk in justice and peace. Fill us with compassion for all your creatures and teach us to live in appreciation of our interrelatedness.

Scripture reflection:

"Come to me, all you that are weary and are carrying heavy burdens, and I will give you rest." Matthew 11:28

Station Six

Veronica wipes the face of Jesus

We adore you, O Jesus, who formed us in love and calls us to follow you.

Jesus speaks:

The brave Veronica comes with her towel to give me comfort and support. The suffering evident on my face calls her compassionate heart to step forth from the crowd. She does not hesitate to consider any possible condemnation of her action by the powerful or the loss of approval from her friends. Her integrity is independent of the fear of consequences; I am grateful for her courage to respond to my needs.

We respond:

Forgive us, O merciful God, when we fail to lessen the agony and tribulation we see in our brothers and sisters. Teach us to engage our hearts and minds to find solutions for the distress we cause to your creation by our turning away from the courage we need to make difficult decisions.

Scripture reflection:

"And whatever you do, in word or deed, do everything in the name of the Lord Jesus, giving thanks to God the Father through him." Colossians 3:17

Station Seven

Jesus falls the second time

We adore you, O Jesus, who formed us in love and calls us to follow you.

Jesus speaks:

O my God, as I fall again I am tormented by my failure to bring abundance of life to all you have claimed as your own. How I tried to help them understand the immensity of your Being; how I hoped they would at least catch a glimpse of the intensity of your unconditional love that burst into glory as stars and planets, sun and moon. From the depths of my joy in knowing you, I desired that your creatures would rejoice in your constant embrace and live their lives in the fullness of union with each other.

We respond:

O loving Creator, teach us to reject our puny and punitive images of you. Forgive us for daring to think we could decide who is worthy to serve and who is welcome at your table. Forgive us for neglecting our responsibilities to all you have made and continue to sustain. May we revere your Sacred Presence everywhere as we rise again to walk with you.

Scripture reflection:

"I came that they may have life, and have it abundantly." John 10:10b

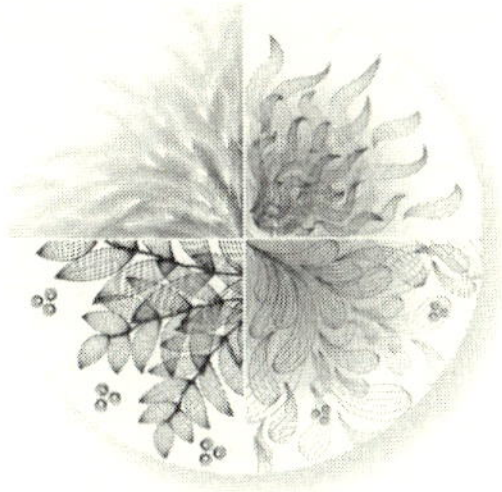

Station Eight

Jesus meets the women of Jerusalem

We adore you, O Jesus, who formed us in love and calls us to follow you.

Jesus speaks:

My beloved daughters, I weep with you as we share the pain of rejection. My message of inclusive love threatened those who held the power to dismiss, erase, and deny my truth. You, created in your Maker's image, have suffered from the beginning of time under a false curse. I treasure your value and I promise to walk with you as you continue to be my faithful disciples. Do not fear to proclaim my good news as you strive to invite my people to remove all divisions and learn to work together to save each other.

We respond:

O Jesus, teach us, your sons and daughters, to bow to the reality of your Divine Spirit alive in everyone. Help us to be grateful that you embrace all discerning hearts and give each person the gifts they need to speak your truth to all who seek you. Give us the vision to walk together as equals in the reign of God, respecting each other's journey and caring for our common home.

Scripture reflection:

"So [the Creator] created humankind in [God's] image, in the image of God [the Holy One] created them; male and female [God] created them." Genesis 1:27

Station Nine

Jesus falls the third time

We adore you, O Jesus, who formed us in love and calls us to follow you.

Jesus speaks:

I grieve for so much darkness in this world of yours, my God. I thought that I could bring light and new life but I see failure all around me. So many of your children struggle with doubt, despair, and loss of hope. Those who labor for peace and justice face obstacles that seem immovable. The voices of those who work to reverse the destructive decisions causing catastrophic changes to your creation are dismissed. I understand why quitting seems like a reasonable response in the face of so much defeat.

We respond:

O Jesus, we watch your determination to rise again. We pray that you will strengthen us to continue standing with those who protest injustice and hatred. We beg you to help us speak truth against the false arguments that prolong the violence bringing so much sorrow into our lives. Lift us up so that we will see the glory of creation and be inspired to protect our fragile earth.

Scripture reflection:

"Then Jesus said…'If you continue in my word, you are truly my disciples; and you will know the truth, and the truth will make you free.'" John 8:31–33

Station Ten

Jesus is stripped of his garments

We adore you, O Jesus, who formed us in love and calls us to follow you.

Jesus speaks:

As I am stripped naked I tremble in humiliation before the eyes of my accusers. Yet I know that I am clothed in love by the Spirit alive within me. I mourn for those who are stripped of their dignity by hatred, misunderstanding, and flawed judgments. I weep for women stripped of their opportunities to share their value. All are precious to me simply because they are mine. I long for the day when everyone will be one in me, living in the shelter of God's womb.

We respond:

We cry at the sight of your shame. Your Sacred Presence within each person commands our recognition that we are all temples of the Divine Spirit. God's blessing song that brought all life into existence invites us to remember that Love created all that is. Have mercy on us for scorning the treasures we have been given and forgive our sinful denials of the many ways we have raped your creation.

Scripture reflection:

"All mine are yours, and yours are mine; and I have been glorified in them. And now I am no longer in the world, but they are in the world, and I am coming to you. Holy Father, protect them in your name that you have given me, so that they may be one, as we are one." John 17:10–11

Station Eleven

Jesus is nailed to the cross

We adore you, O Jesus, who formed us in love and calls us to follow you.

Jesus speaks:

Each excruciating blow of the hammer confirms that I have no escape. Conviction and punishment are how the powerful control those who threaten them with truth, especially the truth of my unconditional love. Too many who seek to be in charge prefer to rule by fear of judgment by a law-giver God, whereas my new reign of God is described by loving, caring, and welcoming. But those who speak of my inclusive way of love are dismissed as betrayers or censored as traitors. And those who dare to teach that we are blessed rather than cursed are silenced.

We respond:

Help us, O Jesus, to live with confidence in the loving God you made real in our world. When we meet unjustified criticism and are wrongly judged, help us trust in your vision leading us to a new path. Encourage us to live boldly as we ask questions in the pursuit of truth. Give us the courage to live without fear and to be willing to pay the price of being your disciples.

Scripture reflection:

"Then justice will dwell in the wilderness, and righteousness abide in the fruitful field. The effect of righteousness will be peace, and the result of righteousness, quietness and trust forever." Isaiah 32:16–17

Station Twelve

Jesus dies on the cross

We adore you, O Jesus, who formed us in love and calls us to follow you.

Jesus speaks:

I look down at my mother being comforted by John. I hear the convicts on either side of me as the crowd is yelling with satisfaction. They do not know what they have done. I think of all those condemned to die: babies by abortion; the just and the unjust in war; the innocent and the guilty by the death penalty. I am aware that my death is imminent; as darkness overwhelms me, I search for you, my God. Where are you? Why have you abandoned me? In spite of your apparent absence, I cling to a desperate hope that you will bring me to new life. I give you my last breath. The soldier plunges his sword into my side.

We respond:

O Jesus, tested by darkness and deprived of God's consolation, you still believed that God was present and would resurrect you to new life. When loss, pain, and injustice threaten our faith in you, strengthen and nourish our hope in your never-failing concern for us. Teach us how to choose life and to cease inflicting death on our brothers and sisters; help us to find ways to preserve and care for your creation as we learn how to stop destroying our common home.

Scripture reflection:

"Restore us, O Lord of hosts, let your face shine, that we may be saved." Psalm 80:19

Station Thirteen

Jesus is taken down from the cross

We adore you, O Jesus, who formed us in love and calls us to follow you.

Jesus speaks:

As my lifeless body is being held by my mother, she trembles with grief as memories from my childhood flood her soul. Numbed by sorrow, her faith is unable to feel my presence enfolding her. I think of all those who suffer anguish and think they are alone. I want to comfort them and assure them that I will never leave them. I will strengthen their broken hearts as they learn to live again. Love never ends and the journey continues.

We respond:

Death plunges us into depths of darkness; dreams and hopes evaporate into the emptiness swallowing our souls. We beg you, O living God, to teach us to believe when we cannot see, to hope in spite of all evidence to the contrary, to love when all seems futile. In your Sacred Presence we lift up all that is lost because you promise resurrection. As we reverence the cycle of life in all creation, help us mourn what is extinct because of our sinful neglect.

Scripture reflection:

"We are afflicted in every way, but not crushed; perplexed, but not driven to despair; persecuted, but not forsaken; struck down, but not destroyed; always carrying in the body the death of Jesus, so that the life of Jesus may also be made visible in our bodies." 2 Corinthians 4:8–10

Station Fourteen

The body of Jesus is placed in the tomb

We adore you, O Jesus, who formed us in love and calls us to follow you.

Jesus speaks:

My human journey is finished; Joseph wraps my body in a linen cloth and carries it to his own tomb. My mother and women disciples from Galilee including Magdalene promise to return with spices and ointments. As they walk away in silence, as people do after burials, my Divine Spirit holds their grieving hearts shattered by questions and doubts. The shadows surrounding them hide the truth of how close I am.

We respond:

O crucified Jesus, as your followers we know that our human journey will also bring us unjustified trials, suffering, and punishments. Life that is treasured will end and our bodies will return to the earth. All of creation moans as death claims what is temporary, so that transformation can give birth to new life beyond our imagining. We are grateful for the hope that sustains us and all you have made.

Scripture reflection:

"But just as we have the same spirit of faith that is in accordance with scripture—'I believed, and so I spoke'—we also believe, and so we speak, because we know that the one who raised the Lord Jesus will raise us also with Jesus." 2 Corinthians 4:13–14

Station Fifteen (optional)

Jesus rises to new life

We adore you, O Jesus, who formed us in love and calls us to follow you.

Jesus speaks:

The women are coming as they promised, carrying spices and perfumed ointments. They are surprised to see that the stone had been rolled away from the tomb. Trembling, they approach and look inside; I am not there! They bow in terror to two men in dazzling clothes and hear words that seem impossible to believe. They run to tell my other disciples, but the women's story is too much for them to believe. Peter and John come to see for themselves. Mary refuses to leave. I find her weeping, and then we celebrate my new life with unbounded joy, but the world is waiting. I tell her that she must go and preach the good news!

We respond:

We thank you, Jesus, and praise you for your witness to the power of the Divine Mystery in each of us, and we bow to your glorious presence everywhere. Teach us how to be your faithful followers, to live in love, always open to new life in the Spirit. We rejoice in hope and ask that you teach us how to live resurrection in communion with you and all of creation.

Scripture reflection:

"And he said to them, 'Go into all the world and proclaim the good news to the whole creation.'" Mark 16:15

Final prayer

We give thanks, O God, for sending Jesus to teach us how to live and how to die. You promise us abundant life and invite us to live believing that you created us as a blessing. Help us to follow your Son, aware that our journey is also his way of the cross and his rising to new life is our assurance of transformation. We bow in adoration to your Sacred Presence holding us and all of creation in your eternal loving embrace. Amen